The Gift of
Marriage

Written and compiled by
Marion Stroud

UPPER
ROOM BOOKS

Together

The Lord God said,
'It is not good for the man to live alone.
I will make a suitable companion
to help him.'

THE BOOK OF GENESIS

Marriage is given,
that husband and wife may comfort and
help each other,
living faithfully together
in need and in plenty,
in sorrow and in joy.
It is given,
that with delight and tenderness
they may know each other in love,
and, through the joy of their bodily union,
may strengthen the union
of their hearts and lives.

THE MARRIAGE SERVICE

Marriage Is...

Marriage is a dynamic process of discovery.

Marriage is a journey, not an arrival.

In marriage, being the right person is as important as finding the right person.

Marriage is starting to love, over and over again.

Marriage is a life's work.

Marriage is an art . . . and like any creative process, it requires active thought and effort. We have to learn how to share on many different levels. We need to practice talking from the heart, and understanding attitudes as well as words. Giving generously and receiving graciously are talents that are available to anyone. But all these skills need to be developed, if the marriage picture that we paint is to be anything approaching the masterpiece that God intended.

All He Ever Dreamed

God,
let me be all he ever dreamed
of loveliness and laughter.
Veil his eyes a bit
because
there are so many little flaws;
somehow, God,
please let him see
only the bride I long to be,
remembering ever after —
I was all he ever dreamed
of loveliness and laughter.

RUTH BELL GRAHAM

I Choose You

'I take you . . . to have and to hold, for better, for worse, for richer for poorer, in sickness and in health . . .'

'These two have come,' he said, 'to promise to face the future together, accepting whatever . . . may lie ahead . . . Nothing is easier than saying words. Nothing is harder than living them day after day. What you promise today must be renewed and redecided tomorrow and each day that stretches out before you. At the end of this ceremony, legally you will be man and wife, but still you must decide each day that you want to be married.'

'Will you take this woman to be your wife?' the minister asked. 'I will,' the boy said, and to the same question, the girl gave the same answer. 'I give you this ring,' the boy said. 'Wear it with love and joy. I choose you to be my wife, this day and every day.'

'I accept this ring,' she replied. 'I will wear it with love and joy. I choose you to be my husband this day and every day.'

'I take you . . . to love and to cherish. With my body I honour you. All that I am, I give to you. All that I have, I share with you, within the love of God.'

Love is not the feeling of a moment, but the conscious decision for a way of life.

Becoming One

It's all very well for them to say that it's in the Bible, but what did God mean by it? How can two people become one person? The joining of our bodies in physical love produces a fleeting oneness — and that can be fantastic. But most of the time we are just two people who love one another, but are so very different. We have different jobs, different likes and dislikes, different abilities and very different ways of doing things.

So if we are to be 'one', which 'one' are we going to be? I certainly don't want to fade out as an individual — not to be 'me' any more. That makes marriage sound like a take-over bid! But perhaps it is not meant to be a take-over so much as a merger. A fusion of our lives, so that one person's weaknesses are compensated for by the other person's strengths; an adding-to rather than a taking-away, for both of us. Rather than cramping and confining us, perhaps this oneness is intended to bring a new dimension to our lives. For if we are secure in the certainty of each other's love and understanding, maybe we can enjoy a special kind of freedom. The freedom to fulfill our potential; to live life to the full in a way that we could never do alone.

Love: A Way of Life

Love is patient and kind; it is not jealous or conceited or proud; love is not ill-mannered or selfish or irritable; love does not keep a record of wrongs; love is not happy with evil, but is happy with the truth. Love never gives up; and its faith, hope, and patience never fail.

PAUL: FROM THE NEW TESTAMENT

We love because God first loved us.

JOHN: FROM THE NEW TESTAMENT

Love is not a single act, but a climate in which we live, a lifetime venture in which we are always learning, discovering, growing.
It is not destroyed by a single failure, or won by a single caress.
Love is a climate – a climate of the heart.

ARDIS WHITMAN

Making the Break

*D*ear Mum

I came home this afternoon; home for good. We had another row – about money this time – and I slammed out of the flat, saying that I wasn't coming back. But you were out. Waiting, I curled up in my old room, and as I wept I remembered . . . you, helping me with my wedding dress, and your final few words as you fixed my veil.

'There'll always be a welcome here for you,' you said. 'But from now on your home is with your husband, and he must come first in your life and loving. If there are problems that you both want to discuss, then we'll be glad to help, but there'll be no welcome for tale telling and no taking sides.'

Was it hard to say that, and harder still to do it – when I was still clinging on, wanting the best of both worlds? Thank you for caring enough to cut me loose. The peace and order in your home has brought life into focus. I've gone back now to get things put to rights in mine.

Today

If we knew that life would end tomorrow, would we still waste today on our quarrels? Would we fritter the precious hours away, taking refuge behind that wall of icy silence, creeping out only to hurl another barrage of angry words – invisible missiles, but in every way as deadly as broken bricks or bottles?

If we knew that life would end tomorrow, would we keep a tally of wrongs, determined not to be the first one to give in? Or would we cease to care who had started it, knowing that no one is completely in the right, and that in this kind of war we shall both end up as losers?

If we knew that life would end tomorrow, surely we would treasure today. Fill the hours to the brim with love and laughter instead of anger and bitterness, creating jewel-bright memories which would lighten our hearts instead of dark regrets which could twist and destroy.

If we knew that life would end tomorrow . . . but who can say that it will not? The only time of which we can be certain is today. So today I will reach out for your hand. Today I will say 'I'm sorry' and 'I love you'.

Forgive and Forget

There is no hope for happiness in harboring hurt feelings or thoughts. In marriage of all places we cannot live in the past. We must, if we are to be happy together, learn the discipline of forgiving and forgetting. In marriage we cannot allow ourselves to be chained to yesterday's mistake or last year's failure. Bridges must be burned, and with God's help they can be.

JOHN DRESCHER

Be humble and gentle. Be patient with each other, making allowance for each other's faults because of your love . . . Don't let the sun go down with you still angry — get over it quickly . . . Quarrelling, harsh words, and dislike of others should have no place in your lives. Instead, be kind to each other, tenderhearted, forgiving one another, just as God has forgiven you . . .

PAUL: FROM THE NEW TESTAMENT

Each Other

Husbands, show the same kind of love to your wives
as Christ showed to the church when he died for her . . .
That is how husbands should treat their wives,
loving them as part of themselves.
No one hates his own body
but lovingly cares for it . . .
So . . . a man must love his wife
as part of himself.

PAUL: FROM THE NEW TESTAMENT

A good wife . . .
is worth more than precious gems!
She is a woman of strength and dignity,
and has no fear of old age.
When she speaks, her words are wise,
and kindness is the rule for everything she says.

THE BOOK OF PROVERBS

The Gift of Words

Thank you, God, for teaching us to talk to one another. Thank you for the gift of words.

Thank you for giving us each other with whom to share our hopes, our fears, our problems and our plans. Banish our fear of ridicule or rejection, so that we can be totally honest, completely ourselves.

Thank you for showing us the need to listen. To listen with our hearts as well as with our ears, sensing the needs that may remain unspoken. To know that when there are no words to meet the situation, then love can be a silent song — a touch that says 'I'm in this situation with you,' a smile that reassures, 'You're doing fine.'

Thank you that we have learned the need for patience. Thank you for teaching a talkative partner brevity, and a quieter one how to express himself.

We often struggle with this vital task of real communication. But thank you God for teaching us to talk to one another. Thank you for the gift of words.

Welcome Home

I thought our home should be properly furnished before others could feel at home.

You said 'Come any time' and when they did, sat them on the floor without a qualm. And the house was properly furnished – with people, with love and with laughter.

I thought that everyday food was for family only; that meals I could offer to guests must have hours of planning and preparation.

You said, 'It will be pot-luck, but you're welcome to share what we have.'

I thought overnight guests were rare creatures, whose coming was a special event.

You said, 'We have an empty bed; stay as long as you need to.'

I thought that our home was our castle.

You said, 'Let down the drawbridge. Having a home is a miracle to be shared.'

Take Time

'*Today we're going out!*' *you said. 'The jobs can wait. It's time we enjoyed ourselves.*'

And so we pushed the washing back into the basket, closed the door on that half-decorated bedroom and left our work-a-day selves behind in the cupboard with the tool-box!

What made today so special? Wandering hand in hand through the quietness of the cathedral cloisters? Laughing at the antics of the ducks as we scattered the remains of our lunch on the river? Finding that book we've always wanted at the back of the market-stall? Or was it just the sunshine that seemed to turn our world to gold?

Perhaps it was all of those things — and yet none of them. Today was special because we took time. Time to talk; time to find out what we were thinking and why; and time to remember that marriage may be hard work, but it's also intended to be fun!

Learning About Love

A *child's most basic security is in knowing that his parents love each other. It is even more important than their love for him. He feels assured of being part of a strong, satisfying relationship and is certain that he'll never be abandoned . . .*

The only people who really know how to express love are those who have seen love expressed. A child knows his parents more intimately, more honestly than anyone else in his life. Therefore, what he is going to learn about love will come from watching them, day after day.

J. ALLAN PETERSEN

Roots and Wings

*O*ur baby has received so many lovely gifts, each one a token of the joyful welcome that exists for him. But there are vital things that he will need that money cannot buy, and loving hands can never manufacture. Please show us, God, how we can give those precious but invisible gifts – roots and wings; security and freedom.

We know that he will need to feel secure; to sense that we will always love him come what may. But we're just human beings – beginners in the school of parenthood. There may be times when we don't feel so loving, when daily life is just too 'daily' and the fabric of our family life gets frayed around the edges. Help us to know that if human parents get it wrong from time to time, we can all depend completely on our Heavenly Father.

The freedom bit is harder. There are so many dangers all around him. Our instinct is to mould and train; to shelter and protect. But in the midst of all our caring help us to free him to be himself; to grow into that special person you have planned for him to be, not some pale imitation of another. Enable him to discover his own gifts and develop them fully. And when we have done all we can, give us the courage to stand aside and let him fly, knowing that your arms will be beneath him wherever he goes.

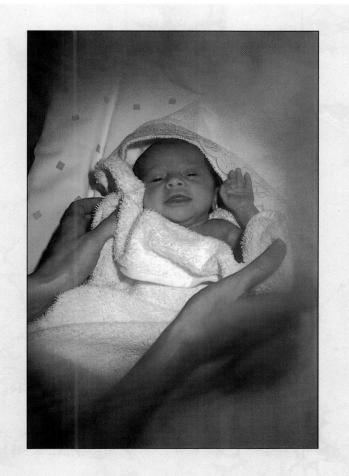

A Walled Garden

**My sweetheart, my bride, is a secret garden, a
walled garden, a private spring . . .**

SONG OF SONGS

'Your marriage,' he said, 'should have within it, a secret and protected
place, open to you alone. Imagine it as a walled garden, entered by a door to
which you only hold the key. Within it you will cease to be a mother, father,
or any other of the roles which you fulfill in daily life. Here you are simply
two people who love each other, concentrating on each other's needs.'

And so we made our walled garden. Time that was kept for us alone. At first
we went there often, enjoying each other's company, sharing secrets, growing
closer. But now our days are packed with plans and people. Conversation has
become a message scribbled on a pad. The door into our garden is almost
hidden by rank weeds of busyness. We claim we have no time because we
have forgotten. Forgotten that love grows if it is tended, and if neglected, dies.
But we can always make the time for what is most important in our lives.

So take my hand and let us go back in to our garden. The time we spend
together is not wasted but invested. Invested in our future and the nurture
of our love.

The Good Days of Marriage

*D*ear Lord, thank you for the good days of marriage. The days when we wake up pleased with each other, our jobs, our children, our homes and ourselves.

Thank you for our communication – the times when we can really talk to each other; and the times when we understand each other without so much as a gesture or a word.

Thank you for our companionship – the times when we can work together at projects we both enjoy. Or work in our separate fields and yet have that sense of sharing that can only come when two people's lives have merged in so many other ways, so long. Thank you for our times of privacy. Our times of freedom. Our relaxed sense of personal trust. Thank you that we don't have to clutch and stifle each other, that we have learned to respect ourselves enough to respect the other's individuality.

Thank you, Lord, that despite the many storms of marriage we have reached these particular shores.

MARJORIE HOLMES

The Best is Yet to Come

Grow old along with me!
The best is yet to be,
The last of life for which the first was made.
Our times are in His hand
Who saith 'A whole I planned,'
Youth shows but half; trust God: see all,
nor be afraid.

ROBERT BROWNING

A Marriage Feast

Fast from criticism and feast on praise,
Fast from self-pity and feast on joy,
Fast from ill-temper and feast on peace,
Fast from resentment and feast on contentment,
Fast from pride and feast on humility,
Fast from selfishness and feast on service,
Fast from fear and feast on faith.